CW00506949

# Outback Pubs
# of Australia

# Outback Pubs
# of Australia

## Rex Newell

### Text by Jill Bowen

The Stop Over Pub (page 110).

C&A CHILD & ASSOCIATES
AN ALL-AUSTRALIAN PUBLISHER

Dedicated to my three sons, Kevin, Tim and Lloyd,
and my late father.

Published by
Child & Associates Publishing Pty Ltd,
9 Clearview Place, Brookvale, NSW, Australia, 2100
A wholly owned Australian publishing company
This book has been edited, designed and typeset in
Australia by the Publisher

First Edition 1987

Text by Jill Bowen
Paintings by Rex Newell
© Paintings Rex Newell 1987
© Text Child & Associates 1987

Typesetting processed by Deblaere Typesetting Pty Ltd
Printed in Australia by The Griffin Press

**National Library of Australia
Cataloguing-in-Publication data**

Newell, Rex, 1938-
    Outback pubs of Australia.

    ISBN 0 86777 155 0.

    1.  Hotels, taverns, etc. —Australia. 2.  Hotels, taverns,
        etc. — Australia — Pictorial works. I. Bowen, Jill.
        II. Title.

647'.949401

# Contents

# Introduction

Australians since the earliest days have loved both a drink and the places that provided a drink.

Not that our earliest pubs, notably those of the bush, could have been described as attractive or pleasant places. Perhaps the word 'vile' would be more accurate.

They were rough grog shanties serving the needs of drovers, teamsters, prospectors and other travellers. Drunken brawls were commonplace. Men went on the ran-tan, ran amok, and some even died.

Some shanty proprietors kept an eye on the less competent of the drinkers with a grave ready-dug for them if the worst seemed likely—especially in the searing summer heat. It is not surprising that some died, considering the snake juice dispensed to them. More than half the contents of a flagon of spirits would be removed, topped up with water and to restore colour to the adulterated drink, old clay tobacco pipes were boiled and the nicotine-laced water was added along with a dash of turps. If beer went flat, it gained an unexpected froth from a bar of soap shaken up in the keg. Some old bushmen maintain that things have improved since. They now have bush champagne ... metho and Epsom salts, and, if pink champagne is desired, 'a slug of beetroot juice can be whacked in'!

Hotels of substance started to appear in the bush in the 1850s as inland expansion intensified and gold discoveries were made. Some of them are still standing today, among the almost six thousand pubs in Australia that cater for just on 16 million Australians. (If this seems high, consider the ratio last century—we had less than half the number of people and almost double the number of pubs!)

It is our pubs, particularly those in the bush, that have fascinated Rex Newell for almost twenty years. He has painted them with some urgency ... mainly because the grand old buildings were disappearing so fast and he wanted to get to them before the demolishers.

Rex Newell was born in Coffs Harbour, New South Wales, in 1938 and grew up in the Kempsey area. He discovered a talent for sketching as a young boy. At the age of fourteen, he'd finished an afternoon's painting on the banks of the Macleay River when a man stopped to admire his efforts on the still-wet canvas and was so taken with the result that he bought the painting on the spot for £3 10s. It firmed Newell's resolve on an art career. He came to Sydney and undertook five years' study in fine art, commercial art and sign-writing. Apprenticeship over, he returned to Kempsey and commercial art and sign-writing—and hated it.

Against expert advice he decided to go it alone as an artist. It was the bush that beckoned, and in particular the pubs. Why pubs?

'Because every time you drive into a town you invariably notice the pubs,' Newell says. 'They're always a focal point in any community. In many country towns the most majestic building is often the old pub. They're social centres that can serve as a post office, a bank, an opal exchange, a debt-collecting agency, a fighting arena; they're also the venue for chook raffles, loud music and some of the best yarns I've ever heard.'

Publicans, says Newell, can be as varied as the pubs. 'In country towns they're quite important blokes. They cash cheques, carry a lot of drinkers and sometimes handle more money than banks. I've known quite a few who were caught by their own medicine.' Not averse to a drink himself, Newell usually makes a bee-line for the nearest pub whenever he hits a town. Largely dependent on local knowledge, he asks about old or quaint hotels in the area. His jovial, outgoing manner usually ensures that he gets the information he wants but at times he's aroused suspicion.

'I don't seem to fit the bush people's image of a painter,' he said. 'They seem to believe that all painters are bearded unwashed hippies. No matter what I say, they prefer to think I am a tax investigator or a copper.'

And on one occasion he has been called something less flattering than that. As Newell tells it: 'I was going around the outback in a light plane. We had to undertake an emergency landing at Milparinka, New South Wales. We didn't have permission to land and saw what appeared to be a landing strip on the road. We decided to go in and as the wheels touched down, stones flew everywhere—into the Piper Arrow's screen, propeller and fuselage. As we stopped, still terrified, we saw a station wagon hammering towards us in a cloud of dust and I thought, "Strike, we're going to cop it," and as I fell out of the plane, a big red-faced bloke got out, shook his fists at us and hollered, "I reckoned if you two dills didn't kill yourselves landing you'd need a beer. Hop in — I'm the publican!"'

In his bid to document Australia's pubs on canvas, Rex Newell has travelled some 250 000 kilometres around Australia and if one thing puzzles him about pubs, it is the dullness and predictability of their names. 'I don't know why Australia is crammed with Lyceums, Post Offices, Railways, Commercials, Tatts, Criterions, Royals and Bridges,' he says.

Some of the pubs that break the dreary name barrier include the Kangaroo at Maldon, Victoria, the Thirst Quencher at Girilambone, New South Wales, the Wellshot at Ilfracombe, Queensland, the Wobbly Boot at Boggabilla, New South Wales, the Blue Heeler at Kynuna, Queensland and the Linga Longa at Gundy, New South Wales.

Newell doesn't know why we don't have some pubs called the Bogged Inn, the Swaggie's Rest, the Miners' Retreat, the Bull's Roar, the Galah's Inn, the Fly on the Wall, the Punters' Haven, the Raw Prawn and ... why not, the Brahms and Liszt?

Rex Newell is a Sydney-based artist and his own favourite watering hole is the 'Harbord Hilton', otherwise known as the Harbord Beach Hotel.

He lives and works close by and if stuck for inspiration when painting or when wanting a short break, goes out on to his balcony which has impressive views of the beach and ocean. Some might say that in travelling and painting the outback and living in Sydney by the sea that Rex Newell has the best of both worlds!

THE NEW ETTAMOGAH PUB

## The Ettamogah Pub, Albury, New South Wales

Created over forty years ago by the cartoonist, Ken Maynard, the Ettamogah Pub has recently come to life near the New South Wales town of Albury. The ricketty facsimile of Maynard's fictitious watering hole was officially opened in May 1987. Built by Albury vigneron, Lindsay 'Coop' Cooper, it remains faithful to the original—there's even a 1929 Chevrolet utility on the roof. Legend has it that the ute ended up there during the great flood of 1946.

The pub is aptly named— Ettamogah is an Aboriginal word meaning a 'good place to drink'. Business is booming at the new pub and customers can even sample a genuine counter lunch, although the chicken legs will have to do as a substitute for emu legs.

# Gilbey's Pub

A fictitious hotel, Gilbey's Pub comes to life for Rex Newell in this poem by his friend 'Dud' Mills. It captures the essence of the Australian bush pub.

## The Ballad of Gilbey's Pub

In a distant mallee scrubland,
To the South of Riverine,
There's a little heap of rubble
Where an old hotel has been
It was shingle roofed and shanty hung
In a 'snake-trap' kind of style,
But the only pub, in that patch of scrub,
You'd find for many a mile.

The teams would make for the kindly light
That glimmered across the track,
And the driver's shout brought the team about
To pass by the hitching rack.
The smouldering log was poked again,
To strike a reluctant blaze,
And the billy hung where the black crane swung,
As it did in the good old days.

A mate came out from the firelight,
With a cheerful word to say
And they stacked the yokes by the waggon spokes
Content to call it a day
The leader's bell, with its booming note,
Swung off thru' the mallee scrub,
The feed was right for the team that night,
So they headed for Gilbey's Pub.

The red coals glowed on the blackened hearth,
Warm welcome to those that came
By their devious ways, in the golden days,
The reception was still the same
To the spieler who worked a thimble and pea,
Or a vagrant rouseabout
A teamster man, or a swart Afghan,
Who was headed for Further Out.

Times there were when the rain fell down,
You could measure it by the yard,
The waggons bogged on the black-soil plain,
And the way to the pub was barred.
But the teamsters rallied, as teamsters will,
Hooked on in a double bank,
They cursed the flood, and they spurned the mud
And the language, at least, was frank.

Now the lowan calls, as the daylight dies,
From the lip of his leaf-mould hill,
And the curlews cry where the sandhills lie,
Ere the voice of the bush is still.
The boomers break on the boundless plain
And make for the mallee scrub,
Like silent wraiths as they slowly pass
The site of old Gilbey's Pub.

The memories throng the bush-land grove,
Through the serried ranks of grass,
And the ghost-gums grow where the shy blue doe
With her furtive tread shall pass.
For the travellers now are dead and gone,
And the trucks replace the teams,
The shadows sway in a wild array
From the glare of the headlight beams.

There's a little heap of rubble
To the South of Riverine,
That served its earthly purpose
In the stirring years between,
It's a monument to the by-gone days
In that patch of mallee scrub,
As it stands alone, in lieu of stone,
To the memory of Gilbey's Pub.

From *The Stock Whip and the Spur* by 'Dud' Mills, published by Cudgegong Newspapers Pty Ltd, New South Wales, 1955.

# Gilbey's Pub

# The Singleton Hotel, Singleton, New South Wales

The Gadang Aborigines occupied a portion of the Hunter Valley, near what is now Singleton, before European settlement and the first recorded journey by a European to the area was that of John Howe, chief constable of Windsor, in 1820. Benjamin Singleton, who was a member of Howe's party settled there on a grant of land and in 1836 part of his property became the town of Singleton. In 1827 Benjamin Singleton built the first inn in the district giving it the attractive name of the Barley Mow. By 1841 some ninety houses had been built and there were some 430 people providing a good bunch of regulars for the Barley Mow.

These days it is the wineries in the rich Hunter Valley area that tend to get the attention and the dollar (at least from the flocks of tourists), rather than the pubs.

Singleton sits happily on the New England Highway and the Hunter River in the rich and diverse Hunter Valley which boasts everything from fine pastoral properties, noted thoroughbred horse studs, wineries and many fine places that offer tourists and harassed Sydneysiders a superb weekend away from the pent-up tensions of the big smoke. The area now has some delightful guest houses (some built in the old colonial style) with their big drawcards being their dining rooms.

Pubs insist they still do quite nicely, thank you, whenever polo tournaments, cattle sales and country attractions are held.

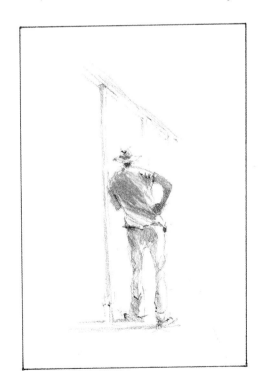

# The Singleton Hotel

# The Commercial Hotel, Hebel, Queensland

No one can dispute the claim that the Commercial is the leading hotel in Hebel, Queensland—the town has only one pub!

A tiny town in sheep country, Hebel nestles just over the Queensland-New South Wales border where the Castlereagh Highway finishes. The pub is more than a hundred years old and aside from a few alterations to the bar, is still in its original state.

Shearers and graziers have always been patrons of the pub which now draws truckies and tourists in increasing numbers. Frequently the tourists are from the south and specifically in the area on fishing trips for the yellow belly and cod in the Narran and Culgoa Rivers. Naturally the bar is never short on tall 'fish stories' and also yarns about the past involving Captain Moonlight who was known to frequent the area in his heyday.

Plenty of swilling of XXXX goes on within the walls of this pub and Rex Newell was wondering if a poem pinned up in the bar gives an inkling as to why ...

> Uncle George and Aunty Mable
> Fainted at the breakfast table.
> This should have been sufficient warning
> Not to do it in the morning.
> XXXX beer has put them right
> Now they do it morn' and night;
> And Uncle George is hoping soon
> To do it in the afternoon.

# The Commercial Hotel

# The Corio Hotel, Goolwa, South Australia

In 1857 the steamer *Corio* was stranded at the mouth of the River Murray and all attempts to refloat her failed.

The vessel was sold the following year to Port Adelaide interests. Sailors from the Port aided by a paddle tug refloated and towed away the unfortunate steamer and the hotel, built and licensed in the same year as the *Corio* was refloated, is believed to have taken its name from that vessel.

An impressive pub at Railway Terrace, Goolwa, on the main highway between Strathalbyn and Victor Harbour, it is built from limestone with a galvanised iron roof.

Of much interest to visitors are the Yankee Doodle ceiling posters inside the pub. How they become a part of the hotel's history is something of a mystery but they stem from an American picture titled *Yankee Doodle* which depicted the Fourth of July celebrations in a humorous style. An American photographer and art dealer saw the oil painting and asked the artist to paint another with a more patriotic flavour. The artist set to work and colour reproductions of the painting, such as those on the ceiling of the Goolwa pub, were sold prior to its exhibition in the Centennial Exposition of 1876 in Philadelphia, its title having been changed from *Yankee Doodle* to *The Spirit of '76*. It has since been described as 'the most patriotic painting in America', showing, as it does, three generations of patriots.

The original painting is now on display in America in the Town Fathers' Meeting Room, Abbot Hall, Marblehead, Massechusetts. How the ceilings of the pub at Goolwa became plastered with the posters more than a century ago is anyone's guess.

The hotel's exterior has remained unchanged. The interior has been revamped to 'pub modern'. As one patron remarked, 'Only a few old things have been retained in the bars ... three old cash registers and the current publican himself.'

# The Corio Hotel

# Newnes Hotel, Newnes, New South Wales

The old mining town of Newnes is on the Wolgan River in the Wolgan Valley or as many would say 'out the back of Lithgow'.

The mining boom is long since over and these days the little single-storeyed timber pub caters for a few locals and visitors, mainly bushwalkers and climbers who are pleased to down their backpacks for a spell in the little pub in a picturesque setting.

When Rex Newell was there his attention was drawn to the poem displayed prominently in the bar:

*A Toast*
The Frenchman drinks his native wine
The German, his Lager Beer.
The Englishman, his half and half
Because it gives more cheer.
The Scotchman drinks his whisky neat
The Irish like it hot.
The Australian's got no national drink
So he drinks the bloody lot!

The poem seems to have been written by that well-known person 'Anon'. A lot of people have begged to differ about the line relating to the Australians. Others with the names of Campbell, McLeod and McGregor have tried to correct the spelling of the word 'Scotchman' to 'Scotsman', but without success!

'NEWNES BAR'

# Newnes Hotel

# The West End Hotel, Mudgee, New South Wales

In 1828 (one year after the establishment of Mudgee as the second settlement west of the Great Dividing Range) George Cox took up a 995 acre land grant and hung on to it for thirty years when it was sold to John Brooks for £5. Anyone unable to get a mental picture of an acre of land may care to think of it as being the equivalent of four average Sydney suburban blocks. Brooks cleaned up nicely on the land transaction selling it in 1857 to George McQuiggan for £460 and it was McQuiggan who built and opened the West End Hotel as quickly as he could *not* only to capitalise on the predictable thirst of the expanding west but also to provide accommodation for their stock.

Being on the edge of the town, the West End Hotel was a convenient resting place for teamsters: the large slab of land and excellent spelling paddock for horse and bullock teams having a frontage of the banks of the Cudgegong River. Robertson's Produce store opposite the hotel was a handy provider of hay and chaff.

The West End's last licensee was Albert Gentle who closed down the pub in 1923.

After that it became a private home and was later acquired by the Bowen family (who'd been in the area since the 1880s) and they converted it into flats. In 1966 the building was bought by the members of the Mudgee Historical Society and turned into a museum— the Colonial Inn.

The West End Hotel is one that hasn't survived the test of time. Yet it hasn't fallen prey to the wrecker's hammer. The 130-year-old former pub now houses local history and still does brisk business accommodating and informing interested tourists.

# The West End Hotel

## The Budgee Budgee Hotel, Mudgee, New South Wales

What happens to an old pub when it's no longer needed as a pub? The answer, in the case of the Budgee Budgee is that it is now used as a hayshed.

The small single-storeyed timber pub (at the Junction of the Cassilis and Muswellbrook roads at Mudgee) was built by William Gossage in the 1860s and was a popular spot for the bullock teamsters working in the area.

# The Budgee Budgee Hotel

# The Paragon Hotel, Mudgee, New South Wales

The name Mudgee is Aboriginal for 'nest in the hills'. It is one of Rex Newell's favourite towns. It was special enough for him to leave Sydney to live and work there in the 1970s. Sydney was too rushed and hectic. There were too many interruptions. He found he could work better in the rural tranquillity Mudgee had to offer.

He set up home base in Mudgee and converted part of the house to a studio and gallery and Mudgee also provided him with the opportunity to conduct his art classes. The classes were large by any standards and saw the group of enthusiasts spend a day or an afternoon on a riverbank tackling perspectives or at a property coming to grips with draughtsmanship by painting rambling old galvanised iron buildings such as the Wilton Woolshed (sadly, this building is now gone).

He recalls with affection his art class (thirty-nine girls aged from twelve to seventy and a Presbyterian minister) springing him with a surprise birthday party on one painting excursion. Not only painting gear was unloaded from the boots of cars but cooked chooks, salads, pavlovas and (ahem) casks of wine. Newell recalls that the class didn't progress very far with painting that day but that it was a totally memorable occasion.

Newell liked Mudgee ... both the people of the town and the handy access the town provided to so many other places of historical interest close by. Mudgee itself provided many handsome old buildings as subjects for painting. One of them was certainly the Paragon pub.

# The Paragon Hotel

# The Maldon Hotel, Maldon, Victoria

Maldon is on the eastern slopes of Mount Tarrangower, 143 kilometres by road north-west of Melbourne. It is a mining, agricultural and pastoral area. Gold was discovered there in 1853 and reef mining was the principal activity from 1856 to the 1920s.

The entire town is classified by the National Trust as one of Victoria's finest examples of the goldmining era.

The town was originally called Tarrangower (after the mountain) but the name was changed to Maldon in 1856 after a town of the same name in Essex, England. The main growth in Maldon took place in the 1860s when many fine buildings were built ... banks, stores, homes and the inevitable hotels— Maldon boasted the incredible number of sixty at one time.

Their presence was quickly offset by the churches establishing themselves around town and Sunday attendance became as much a part of the town's life as the roll-up (and roll-outs) from the pubs.

Some of the pubs, it must be said, were hardly more than a barrel on a counter under a hessian awning.

One of the most famous pubs in Maldon is the Old Kangaroo Hotel where Cobb & Co. had its depot and travelling theatre companies staged their shows for the miners.

# The Maldon Hotel

## Wyndham Hotel, Wyndham, New South Wales

When Rex Newell said he was setting off for Wyndham, any number of his friends wanted to throw farewell parties for him believing that he'd be out of town for several weeks. They also gave him the names and addresses of friends and contacts in Western Australia.

It just goes to show that people are more instantly aware of Wyndham, Western Australia, than they are of the town with the same name in New South Wales, which is almost halfway between Merimbula on the south coast and Bombala, not far from the Victorian border.

The two men in the bar next to Newell at the pub in Wyndham were reading something in a newspaper. On finishing reading the item, one folded the newspaper and announced to the other,

'A pack of lies ...'

'Yeah,' said the second.

'What're the three greatest lies in the world?' the first asked.

'Dunno ...' the second replied.

'Of course I'll respect you in the morning. The cheque's in the mail. I'm a public servant, can I help you?'

Newell hadn't heard the last 'great lie' which gave everyone a good laugh. Rex Newell pledged he wasn't a public servant and would like to help out by shouting them both a drink. It was the start of a very happy stay in Wyndham, New South Wales.

# Wyndham Hotel

# The Hotel National, Normanton, Queensland

With so many nearby buildings painted white and various shades of cream, the Hotel National, Normanton, provides an outstanding splash of colour in the main street. Painted a mauve colour for more than ten years it became popularly known as 'the purple pub'.

This Gulf Country pub is thought to be around ninety years old. In typical outback fashion no one has placed too great an importance on the keeping of records, so its exact age remains unknown.

The National is a blend of two pubs. A corner section is the original hotel built for Chris and Caroline Dooley and the long front section was formerly the Exchange Hotel, Croydon, Queensland, in the goldrush days. It was transported from Croydon and the two buildings moulded together during World War I. Much of the timber and corrugated iron building is still in its original form and the bar and lounge have a good display of old rifles, bottles and Aboriginal artefacts.

When Rex Newell went north to paint the pub, Bill and Lyn Aspinall had had the pub for ten years and although Bill was only in his early fifties, he was known as 'old Bill'.

He presided behind the bar with his own inimitable style of greeting and hospitality much to the amusement of regulars and consternation of visitors. 'What do you want, you bastard?' was Bill's most common greeting. Anything more polite put a worried look on the faces of regulars who wondered if they'd done something to offend or displease, or whether 'Old Bill' was sick!

Bill prided himself on his bar signs: 'In this establishment the customer is NEVER right' and 'Under old management continuing the same, old, lousy service.' Passengers on safari-style bus tours *never* forget a visit to 'the purple pub'.

# The Hotel National

# The Grand Hotel, Kookynie, Western Australia

In the 1890s the bank crashes and Depression had the eastern States of Australia in a vice-like grip. Western Australia was saved from this by the great gold boom. In 1887 gold was discovered at Southern Cross and in 1892 at Coolgardie, Kalgoorlie and Norseman and then to the north at Wiluna and Meekatharra. Ships going to the west were jam-packed (there was no railway line), and men rode horses, donkeys, camels, or walked pushing wheelbarrows, to get to the diggings which included the area of Kookynie, about halfway between Leonora and Menzies.

The lucky ones rode Cobb & Co.—and paid a hefty price for it. In 1896 Cobb & Co. sold its coaching interests to 'cattle king' Sid Kidman for £10 000 and Kidman continued to run it under the name of Cobb & Co. Money seemed no object to people where transport to and from the goldfields was concerned. Some of the coaches carried between twenty and thirty passengers and, in addition, twice a month, transported between half a ton and a ton and a half of gold from the goldfields.

As with diggings elsewhere, shacks soon appeared made from hessian slung on poles, canvas, old packing cases, corrugated iron and beaten-out kerosene tins. As the various areas, including Kookynie grew, they were reorganised into proper towns with the extra-wide streets needed for turning camel teams. Later, if the gold lasted, came fine stone buildings.

In 1905 Kookynie was a thriving mining town of fifteen hundred people, six hotels, electric street lights, public baths, a newspaper and a brewery which sold nearly 400 000 gallons (close to 2 million litres) of beer in ten years and it also had many fine brick buildings. In 1912 the ore ran out, the mines closed and the town declined. The population was thirty in 1950 and reduced to twelve almost twenty years ago. The Grand Hotel, built in 1894 with its big verandahs and five metre ceilings, is a grand reminder of those days.

# The Grand Hotel

## The Tilba Tilba Hotel, Tilba Tilba, New South Wales

Tilba Tilba and Central Tilba are tiny villages in the heart of dairying country on the New South Wales south coast. Central Tilba is made up of about twenty-five timber buildings dating from the 1890s and has been declared a conservation area.

The pub at Tilba Tilba goes to show that dairymen as well as the bushies need a watering hole.

The Tilba Tilba Hotel caught Rex Newell's eye immediately. As well as being a pub to paint, it was also one to have a drink in. Rex likes Tilba Tilba. Now he doesn't tell friends when he's going there because they automatically inundate him with requests for vast loads of cheese, for which the area is renowned.

'THE BEER CART'

# The Tilba Tilba Hotel

## The Walcha Road Hotel, Walcha Road, New South Wales

Someone's matrimonial troubles were surfacing in the bar at the Walcha Road Hotel when Rex Newell called there. Newell wondered whether it might have been the commercial traveller playing up again ...

One fellow, obviously the worse the wear for drink, snarled at his mate ... 'Well, what would *you* do if you came home after a hard day and found a bloke in bed with *your* wife ... ?'

The other fellow knew exactly: 'I'd break his white stick and shoot his guide dog,' he said.

'OLD SWAGGY'

# The Walcha Road Hotel

## The Curlewis Hotel, Curlewis, New South Wales

At the Curlewis Hotel, Rex Newell met the well-known New South Wales pastoralist, Wally Munro in the bar and Munro's mate, a big, burly Queensland grazier, Ranald Chandler. Newell told them he was about the business of painting pubs. Chandler endorsed the pursuit as 'admirable'. Every bush pub, Chandler said, was 'an institution that had its own following and its own personalities', although he felt, it would be hard for any of them to trump Paddy Kelly who was a drinker at Chandler's watering hole, The Shakespeare Hotel at Barcaldine, Queensland.

Chandler told Newell: 'Our Paddy Kelly claims to be a relation of Ned's— he might be too for all I know— and he does a bit of work on the railways living at his navvy's camp out of town. But he didn't escape the mobile chest X-ray unit when it called out there. They caught up with him later and said, "Pat, you've got TB." Paddy yelled at them, "Don't be bloody stupid. I haven't got the power on yet." He'd told us a while back that he was going to get "one of them fancy colour TVs," and we said to him, "Paddy, ya can't get television if you haven't got electricity," and he said, "I'm gittin' a kerosene job." He told us he'd hang on to it for a while and then give it to the nice nurses at the hospital because he was giving up navvying and taking up droving again.

' "Are ya, Pat?" I said to him. "Where're ya goin'?"

'He said, "I'm gittin' a big team of bullocks and I'm takin' 'em right down the Darling across to Tasmania" ... I asked him how he was gunna get across Bass Strait and he said, "I'm not goin' that way ..." '

Newell roared laughing. The pub roared laughing. Chandler asked if there were any such 'personalities' that frequented the Curlewis pub. There were no nominations. No hands went up. It seemed the pub didn't have anyone who could trump Paddy Kelly.

# The Curlewis Hotel

# The One Tree Hotel, One Tree Plains, New South Wales

The One Tree Hotel stands on the long, hot, flat and almost treeless plains known as 'Hell'. It became a watering hole for stockmen, travellers and Cobb & Co. coaches as expansion in south-western New South Wales took place last century. One Tree is about halfway between Hay and Booligal and it was from Booligal that the Cobb & Co. coaches contined north-west to the river port of Wilcannia. Henry Lawson and A. B. Paterson wrote about the pub. Songs have been written including it. Many of them relate to shearing time in the Riverina, when shearers busted their cheques and drank to excess there.

The One Tree Hotel was built by Alex Finch in 1862. It was named after the one solitary tree that stood close by it which continued to remain a most distinguishing feature until New Year's Day 1900 when the one and only tree burnt down. It seems the skullduggery of a drunk was responsible for the demise of the tree.

No one is quite sure why but in 1903 the hotel itself was destroyed by fire. But the prospect of the One Tree Plains without the old watering hole was so unthinkable that it was soon rebuilt in split pine to resemble the original building. In the war year of 1942, the One Tree Hotel was delicensed. When the National Trust was started, it wasted no time in classifying the well-known bush building as being important to our heritage.

'ONE TOO MANY'

# The One Tree Hotel

## The Narromine Hotel, Narromine, New South Wales

'Cripes, we used to have some fun in this bar years ago,' an old-timer told Rex Newell when he was washing down the dust with a beer at the Narromine Hotel. 'The bridal suite used to be right above the bar so we drilled a hole in the ceiling and tied a bit of string to the double bed mattress wires and let 'er down through the ceiling with a cork tied to the end.

'We all used to make bets and stand here waiting to see what time the cork started to bob!'

The city relatives of one Narromine bride, who put up at the pub while they were there for the wedding, were so incensed by the piece of bush vulgarity that they reprimanded the publican—threatening him that his licence stood in question if the distasteful jape did not cease.

'Bloody old spoil sports,' the old-timer sneered at Newell.

'Yeah, mate,' Newell replied. 'The world's full of 'em.'

Narromine was very full of itself in the year of 1901 when its large and splendid hotel was built. No doubt influenced by the great national event of Federation, the pub was initially named the Federal. But forty-seven years and thirteen publicans later, it decided to do away with the name 'Federal' and in 1948 underwent a name change and became the Narromine Hotel. There were numerous other Federal or Federation Hotels scattered throughout Australia and in order to avoid any confusion and to stamp itself with its own special identity, the people of Narromine insisted that their lovely old hotel should take the town's name.

# The Narromine Hotel

# The Bellbrook Hotel, Bellbrook, New South Wales

A small town fifty kilometres from Kempsey on the Macleay River, Bellbrook defies time and change.

The only businesses in the town (which has been classified by the National Trust) are the pub, the police station and lock-up and the general store. To the memory of some visitors, the store has had the same set of four saucepans in the same window display for the past twenty years.

Surrounded by cattle, timber and dairying activities, the only sound that breaks the tranquillity is the occasional bellow of a beast or the burble of the fast-running Macleay River over rocks and stones at the back of the pub.

The pub, which only has a handful of years to go before it notches up its centenary, is well patronised by local people—workers on cattle properties, timbercutters and Aborigines from the nearby Nulla Creek Mission. (Australian entertainer Slim Dusty was reared in the area and went to school at Nulla.) Tourists fishing for bass frequent Bellbrook which is the home of the Bellbrook Wobbler Bass. Such fish have been recorded up to two and a half kilograms in weight with the average hitting the scales at one kilogram or less.

Bellbrook annually draws a crowd at its Yowie Festival on the long weekend in January. Some years ago a local laid claim to having seen a 'Yowie' (a huge, hairy monster supposed to rage in the bush and the local equivalent to the Yeti or Abominable Snowman). After a few beers too many at the Bellbrook, people aren't surprised at anyone alleging to having seen a Yowie. In any case the town has created a festival out of the incident and annually people give themselves over to a Yowie Hunt.

It's held in a carnival atmosphere, along with street running and rodeo events.

# The Bellbrook Hotel

# 'Do I Get Another Beer ...?'

A well-known pub story, often attributed elsewhere, did have its origin at the Bellbrook Hotel. It concerned the teamster travelling from Five Day Creek to Kempsey hauling cedar logs with a bullock team. He reached Bellbrook on the Friday where he holed up for two days, drinking non-stop. At the crack of dawn on the Monday he set about to leave but felt so ill after the two-day bender that he needed a few drinks to straighten him out.

He belted on the publican's door hollering for grog but the publican told him to get lost. He returned some time later hollering for grog again and invited the publican to have a change of heart about serving him. He had hitched up his team and from the log carrier fastened a chain to one of the pub's verandah posts. The teamster stood back and bawled at the publican, 'Do I get another beer— or will I pull your bloody pub down ...?' It should be said that the gravity of the situation was instantly realised by the publican. The teamster was served quickly and smartly.

The incident is featured on the Bellbrook pub T-shirts and has been documented in many journals— only it is a yarn that seems to have lost direction and is often applied to the wrong pub. Bellbrook insists it happened at its pub first.

# The Bellbrook Hotel

# The Bellbrook Snake-Catcher

The most memorable evening Rex Newell ever spent in a pub was one of his old Friday night boyhood haunts, the Bellbrook. He still recalls the occasion with feelings of both alarm— and humour.

When he was there ten years ago, a former schoolfriend, Johnny Barber, walked into the bar. They had not seen each other for years, claimed each other enthusiastically and settled down to yarning and drinking.

Newell informed Barber that he was still hammering the outback, painting the glory of the bush; Barber told Newell he was earning a quid catching snakes and lizards for a reptile park on the central coast of New South Wales. Newell wanted to know how he found the critters.

'It's easy, mate,' Barber replied, 'I just take my shoes off and wade through the swamps near Crescent Head Road. When I feel 'em under m' feet, I grab 'em!'

Drinkers in nearby groups fell silent and listened with awe as Johnny Barber unfolded some of his amazing swamp discoveries— and then excused himself from his friends and left the bar, which at 9 p.m. was at its boisterous best and jam-packed with drinkers.

Barber returned a couple of minutes later with a plastic garbage bin and in his effort to thread it and himself through the crowd, someone knocked the lid off. The shouts and screams were blood curdling. The swearing was spectacular. Men ran in all directions. Some men ran up and down on the spot (getting nowhere fast) as a selection of snakes 'dropped into' the boozing scene unexpectedly. Such was the rush to get out of the place, people dived through windows as well as doors.

Newell, in his standard drinking gear (shirt, shorts and thongs) considered himself particularly vulnerable. On seeing one large carpet snake hit the floor, he showed the pub a clean set of heels. The memory of Johnny 'Snake-catcher' Barber always brings a big grin to his face.

# The Bellbrook Hotel

# The Commercial Hotel, Burra, South Australia

The Commercial Hotel at Burra, is another pub that has clocked up its centenary. This lovely old pub first opened its doors on 1 February 1878 and a hundred years later received considerable publicity, less on account of the hotel's centenary celebrations than for the role it played during the making of the Boer War film, *Breaker Morant.*

Press, film production people and actors mingled with the regulars at the pub; the visitors were amused to learn that the pub was tagged the 'Sheep Shit Hotel' by the locals, rural men in the area being its best customers.

March is the trump trading time of the year when merino studs are open for inspection and the Commercial (plus other pubs over a wide radius) are booked out by graziers from every State.

The hotel is a focal point in Commercial Street, the main business street in the town that lies a hundred kilometres north of the famous Barossa Valley and thirty-eight kilometres north-east of the Clare Valley, another noted wine-growing area.

The building is small, two-storeyed, built from local stone and capped by an iron roof. It is no longer in its original state. Licensees over the years have not been able to resist the temptation of tampering with it. A section of the upstairs verandah has been enclosed with Cooper louvre windows and the impressive stonework at the front of the pub is coated with layer after layer of paint. Despite this, the 'Sheep Shit' still manages to maintain a distinct, old world charm.

'THE BURRA BURRA MINE'

# The Commercial Hotel

# The O'Connell Hotel, O'Connell, New South Wales

The bar in the old O'Connell Hotel is said to have been listed at one stage in *The Guinness Book of Records* as being the shortest in Australia—precisely 11 feet (3.3 metres) in length. Because of this claim to fame the old section has been preserved in a main bar that has been extended considerably.

Originally O'Connell was on the main road from Sydney to Bathurst and from Bathurst to Goulburn. The settlement developed to cater for travellers and also for local farmers. The hotel has been licensed since 1865. It's seen a number of owners since then. Currently the hotel licence is held by Norman Hoadley, a district grazier.

Today, the closely settled rural community who support their local pub have created a happy informal atmosphere which fascinates the increasing number of passing motorists and those tourists interested in country pubs with a history.

'THE BREAKING OF THE DROUGHT'.

# The O'Connell Hotel

# Ravenswood, Queensland

At various stages and at various places in its history, Australia has been a burrower's paradise as people have surged, scrambled and dug for mineral wealth. One such place they set upon in earnest was Ravenswood, the oldest inland town in North Queensland. There, the rush was on for gold.

It had a mining life of fifty years and in that time produced almost 1 million ounces (over 28 million grams) of gold yet never in a steady stream. The town that grew up lurched between extremes of boom and bust.

Pastoralists, keen to expand with stock and always alert to the dirt at their feet, found the first deposits of gold but showed little or casual interest in it. Their destinies lay in frontiers further out. Yet they did encourage experienced prospectors knowing that any goldrush meant a ready local market for their beef. The arrival of diggers meant storekeepers soon followed and by 1875 Ravenswood was a mixture of a canvas city and fledgling town proper with the emergence of some buildings of substance. Evidence of both boom and bust is that the population of the field fell from three thousand in 1871 to eight hundred in 1876 but recovered in succeeding years to the point that between the years of 1902-05 there were almost five thousand people in Ravenswood: a population that would be envied by many outback towns today.

The heady days of the earth yielding gold petered out towards the end of World War I when the population dwindled to below a thousand. It has declined ever since although there was a small revival in the Depression years when two of the big mines were worked and the old tailings of a third mine put through the cyanide vats a second time.

Many of the fine old buildings (timber and iron) lent themselves to relocation and were dismantled and railed out of town ... some to the sugar towns of the coast and others to the west. The ornate brick buildings that reflect the years of extreme prosperity can never be moved and remain as guardians of the past.

# Ravenswood

## The Railway Hotel, Ravenswood, Queensland

These days there is a quiet calm about Ravenswood which is fifty-eight kilometres from Charters Towers towards the coast to Townsville. The cattle business keeps alive the sleepy little town in which fewer than sixty people live and where the mullock heaps, festooned with rubber tree vine, spill down to the main road.

Like the Imperial Hotel at Ravenswood, the Railway Hotel is another excellent example of 'goldfields brash'. It was also built at the turn of the century in the town's heyday by John Moran who, like Jim Delaney the builder of the Imperial, had been very successful earlier in goldmining ventures.

The hotel is about the same size as the Imperial and so similar in style that it is possible that the same architect designed both pubs.

They went in for the removal of buildings in Ravenswood in a big way and Moran's hotel replaced a single-storeyed pub that was moved across the road and used as a photographer's shop.

The School of Arts Hall and Library (more than a century old) still stand, and remain focal points of Ravenswood's social life. St Patrick's Church is the only church left of three that once served the town. Formerly Roman Catholic, it is now used as a community church.

Ravenswood does not lack for tourists ... people genuinely interested in the history of the old gold town. Most make it a 'must' to trek through the old cemetery. It sheds its own light on the town's headier days when nearly five thousand people lived there; most of them caught up in the scratchings and scramblings for gold.

# The Imperial Hotel, Ravenswood, Queensland

At the turn of the century almost five thousand people lived in Ravenswood, Queensland. At the end of World War I the town, once supported by gold mining, had collapsed. Many transportable buildings were moved elsewhere.

The buildings that do remain in the ghost town today give an insight into the better days and former wealth that the town enjoyed.

In the early 1870s Ravenswood was shaping up as Queensland's major inland town. Payable gold had been discovered in the district in 1868 and mining flourished. It was from the wealth gained from his Donneybrook mine that Jim Delaney built his first Imperial Hotel in the late 1890s. One year, and one bad fire later, Delaney was obliged to build another.

He struck out for grandeur this time (or 'goldfields brash' as the style has been tagged). His second hotel was in coral brick and timber with the front fascias all in carved timber. This time he added a second storey with a connecting, handsome spiral cedar staircase.

The old poppet head of a mine stayed adjacent to the pub within five metres of the main bar—a timely reminder of Delaney's earlier lifestyle when he dug for gold rather than served it in liquid form across the bar.

When Rex Newell went to Ravenswood, the pub was still run by the Misses Delaney, the daughters of the original owner who loved yarning about the past. The once palatial pub now has a lack of clientele and as there are insufficient patrons to warrant beer on tap, it is now served in cans and bottles.

'OLD DERRICKS RAVENSWOOD'

# The Imperial Hotel

# Gwalia State Hotel, Gwalia, Western Australia

Governments have been known to spend money in silly, if not amazing ways, and very often government expenditure results in jeers rather than cheers. But there was jubilation in Western Australia soon after the turn of the century when the government of the day announced it would build a string of pubs! As a government-financed and -built pub, it was quite proper that the first hotel at Gwalia, Western Australia, should be named the Gwalia State Hotel.

The substantial two-storeyed brick building was opened in 1903 in order to give the town its first licensed premises and to lessen the sly-grog trade which was rife at the time.

Due to leasehold titles to land at Gwalia, no one would put up the money for a hotel on land that they could not own so although nearby Leonora had seven pubs, Gwalia went without.

The first Labor government in Western Australia decided after much debate, to build a hotel as a State enterprise. This was done at a cost of £6000 and business was so brisk that a much larger bar had to be added within a couple of years. It was said that on a busy night at the Gwalia State, an eighteen gallon keg lasted twenty minutes. Some say the tap was never turned off.

Government officials swooned with delight at the profits which led to the establishment of a whole chain of Western Australia State hotels. They continued as such until the 1950s when under Liberal government policy the hotels were sold to local communities. Gwalia was the last to go. It was sold to the Gwalia Community Hotel Ltd, floated with capital of £1000 subscribed by local residents. However the hotel had only a few more years to go as such and sadly closed its doors early in 1964.

# Gwalia State Hotel

# The Texas Hotel, Texas, Queensland

It was a natural for Rex Newell to hit the Texas Hotel as soon as he drove into the Queensland town.

In the bar he was asked, 'What brings you to our fair town?' It was winter and Newell replied, 'I'm chasing some of your good Queensland sunshine. I'm heading north on a holiday. Taking a bit of a break ...'

'No one round here much takes holidays,' Newell was told.

'Why not?' Newell asked. 'You all look like hard workers.'

'Well, not after what happened to Fred ...'

'What happened to Fred?'

'He went away to the coast with his missus and left Dave in charge of his place and when he came back a few weeks later, he called into the pub here, didn't he, and it was a Saturday arvo and Dave was in the bar. He said to Dave, "How are things at home?" and Dave said, "No good, boss. All the chooks is dead." Fred said, "What do you mean, all the chooks is dead?" and Dave said, "From eating dead horse meat, boss."

' "What the bloody hell were they doing eating dead horse meat?"

' "Stables got burnt down, boss. Burnt the bloody horses."

' "How the bloody hell did the stables burn down ...?"

' "A spark from the house, boss." '

Newell swears that's the reason he was given for the good people around Texas not taking holidays. But he liked the Texas people and the Texas pub and on any journey now from Inverell to Warwick, he always makes a point of calling there, usually to hear this tale recounted to any stranger in the bar.

# The Texas Hotel

## The Tingha Hotel, Tingha, New South Wales

Tingha is an old tin-mining town in north-west New South Wales. The impressive, two-storeyed Tingha Hotel appealed to Rex Newell as soon as he saw it on one of his pub-hunting missions.

'I liked the look of the pub straight away and also some of the other buildings close to it. On the corner of the main street across from the pub was a little old shop titled General Store and Undertaker.

'I ambled over to have a look in the window which displayed a tin of paint that could only be described as historic. I strolled inside to have a further look around and the old gent behind the counter asked if he could assist me and we started chatting, initially about the tin of paint and my curiosity about it as an artist and then about the business he'd been running all his life ... that of general store owner and undertaker of the district.

'The old man seemed glad of the company soon after nine o'clock in the morning and then took me out into a cold, old tin shed at the back of the shop. He showed me six of the coffins he had to offer the relatives of any deceased locals. They ranged from expensive coffins with brass handles (deluxe jobs) down to cheaper versions. The old man was very proud of the skill and craft he'd put into them. As much as it was interesting, the thought of leaving the shed was very appealing. The storekeeper wrapped up our yarn by telling me of the new district hospital that had recently been completed and of the business decline that had accompanied it.

'It must have been shortly after ten o'clock when we went back into the shop and I noticed that the doors of the Tingha pub across the road were open for business. I felt a dose or two of its fortifying "medicine" would stand me in good stead. The pub had looked good to me from the outside. It was even better on the inside!'

# The Tingha Hotel

# The Dora Dora Hotel, Talmalmo, New South Wales

Is it a pub or is it a museum? The answer, where the Dora Dora Hotel is concerned, is that it is both!

The old pub, on the headwaters of the Murray River (not far from Holbrook and Albury) was built more than 135 years ago. It boasts the most fascinating collection of artefacts, memorabilia (and some would say 'junk') that keeps visitors and drinkers enthralled for hours. Everything from rifles and swords to sporting trophies, kitchen utensils, old flags, bottles, shells, musical instruments and hats—including diggers' hats, tin helmets and gas masks.

The collection has been built up over the years (thousands of customers and visitors have contributed) to the point that there is barely a spare sliver of space on the walls, ceilings and verandah.

Because it is so unusual, the Dora Dora pub and its precious collection of bits and pieces have been featured time and time again on television programmes as being an excellent example of an Aussie pub with plenty of character.

# The Dora Dora Hotel

# The Waukaringa Hotel, Waukaringa, South Australia

The ghost town of Waukaringa lies about 200 kilometres west of Broken Hill. The town is deceiving in appearance: it lacks that atmosphere of disrepair and looks for all the world like a thriving outback town.

The old Waukaringa Hotel stands as a monument in stone to this former mining town. Inoperative for more than a decade now, the hotel once catered for workers on the lonely outback stations and the occasional passerby. The publican for many years, Bob de Pury, also ran a store in the town. He seemed quite content with his life here and once proudly claimed to have cleared £2000 in one year.

With de Pury's death came the demise of this historic old hotel and the town of Waukaringa: he was its last inhabitant.

# The Waukaringa Hotel

# The Tibooburra Hotel, Tibooburra, New South Wales

The original meaning for the expression 'back of Bourke', is, literally, anything west of Bourke and, in particular, west of the Paroo River. That includes Tibooburra— noted both for its remoteness and sky-high temperatures in summer. Some still consider it backblocks country and an uninviting place to live or even visit.

It was even less inviting a little more than a century ago yet still managed to draw people in hordes after gold was discovered at Mount Browne in 1881. People poured out of the river ports of Wilcannia and Bourke intent on scratching a fortune from the dirt. But the scene at Mount Browne, and later at Tibooburra when gold was discovered there, was one of despair. There was barely enough fresh water for men and horses to drink let alone wash off the auriferous dirt.

It was the wily old 'cattle king', Sidney Kidman, who set up the first ration store at Tibooburra knowing that the miners would want meat, flour and provisions. The store was an instant success; but the lack of water at Mount Browne and Tibooburra made them tragic places. Men were stricken with sandy blight and died of typhoid and dysentery. Within three years the area had produced about £80 000 worth of gold but at such an alarming cost in money, health and life that the diggers retreated rapidly.

A reporter from the *Age* newspaper, Melbourne, sent to investigate the great gold discoveries at Mount Browne and Tibooburra in 1882 said that he suffered endless days of hell travelling, in a Morrison Brothers coach, through desolate country to reach the goldfields. After Wilcannia the reporter said, the water was scarce and putrid and drinks at the wayside hotels even worse. He preferred to sleep under the stars than to sample their accommodation.

These days things are better. Rex Newell thought the Tibooburra pub a fine watering hole.

# The Tibooburra Hotel

# The old hotel at Wanaaring, New South Wales

The tiny settlement of Wanaaring (it is far too small to be called a town) 1122 kilometres north-west of Sydney had a pub nearly a hundred years before it had power.

Electricity reached Wanaaring in August 1982 and there was much jubilation as the lights went on in the street and the fifteen buildings that made up the small settlement. The population of seventy-five residents stood in the main street cheering and then headed off to the pub for a celebration proper featuring wine glasses stamped with a 'Lights On!' logo. Aside from the lights, quite a few people were nicely lit for the weekend festivities.

As one old-timer remarked, 'We can now hear dogs barking in Wanaaring. Before when the generators were going at the pub, the police station, the general store and the health centre you couldn't hear a thing. It was like having your head in a car bonnet on a corrugated road!'

The pub at Wanaaring these days is the focal point of the town. It is a small modern building with a happy family atmosphere and Friday nights see most of Wanaaring in the pub ... mums, dads, kids in pyjamas and dogs. The visitor is automatically made welcome in this big, extended family out the back of Bourke.

The pub painted by Rex Newell is the old pub at Wanaaring. It went the way of so many bush hotels ... in a fire many years back. But someone showed Newell a picture of the old pub. He thought it smacked of good old-fashioned style and it quickly found its way onto a canvas.

# The old hotel at Wanaaring

# The Dunny Door, Grenfell, New South Wales

It's always the front of the pub that catches the eye. But for twenty years Rex Newell has stomped and tramped their backyards as well— particularly in the bush and either in search of the gents' or to check out the faithfulness of the pub's architecture. Some pubs are architectural frauds ... with a grand old face fronting the street, a swished-up modern interior and a combination posterior view. There is no such pub with the name the Dunny Door, at Grenfell, New South Wales, but Newell felt that the backyard of the Royal Hotel was so typical of so many backyards of bush pubs that he decided to paint the 'backside view' of a pub.

It was done with some purpose. Newell had been asked if he would supply and donate a painting for the Dunny Door Auction which is held once every two years at the town of Winton, central-western Queensland. The Dunny Door paintings are put up for auction in the main street as a major night-time event with proceeds from each painting going to the charity cause nominated by the artist.

Rex Newell painted the rear view of the Royal Hotel, Grenfell, as his contribution to the Winton Dunny Door Auction in 1981. Fellow artists responded on a lighter note. Some painted on old timber dunny lids and seats; others on wrenched-off dunny doors which they covered with redback spiders and other creepy-crawlies. The selection of Dunny Door art which is ultimately up for offer is always little short of remarkable. Newell's effort, painted in his typical style, certainly didn't draw thigh-slapping snorts of laughter from the crowd. It was never intended for this. It did draw the respectful nods of some serious bidders who nominated big money and gave the painting a home in the headquarters' boardroom of a major stock and station agency. Newell asked that funds raised from his painting go to the Stockman's Hall of Fame, an organisation he has helped since its inception. Based in nearby Longreach, Queensland, it pledges to preserve the heritage of the bush— and the bush heroes.

# The Dunny Door

# The Club Hotel, Wilcannia, New South Wales

If there is one word to describe the Club Hotel, Wilcannia, then it is 'lively'. The handsome, two-storeyed sandstone building is one of Wilcannia's earliest, dating back to 1867. The town had its pub before it had a police station, court house or church. The pub met the requirements of all these buildings to the point that a person could be arrested downstairs in the bar for drunkenness, taken to court in a room upstairs and charged, then to church in the room across the hall (for the repenting of sins if need be) then back downstairs to the bar to start all over again. Wilcannia's old records show that quite a few made 'the round trip'!

In dry and dusty western New South Wales, the pub enjoys a good year-round trade boosted especially in the summer months when the mercury rises and the temperatures regularly hit the old fashioned 100°F.

In recent times the pub has had four favourite personalities—Don, Cookie, Snowy and Stinger.

Don has a little mongrel dog that follows him everywhere; Stinger has a lot of chooks that he rounds up with a stockwhip; Snowy follows the horses and knows every Melbourne and Caulfield Cup winner; and Cookie, with an excess of 'singing syrup' regularly falls on his head. His head has had so many stitches that he is often referred to as 'Cricket Ball'. They are four old-timers who enjoy nothing more than a session at the Club and a few South Australian West End beers as they yarn (and argue) about the past.

THE BLUE OUT FRONT

# The Club Hotel

# The Royal Hotel, Hill End, New South Wales

Hill End is a former goldrush town in the Evans Shire 289 kilometres by road west of Sydney. Alluvial gold was discovered there in 1851 and between 1871 and 1874 when the most significant finds (including Holtermann's nugget) were made and the majority of reef mining took place, Hill End experienced a boom. But by 1874 the yields began to decline, mines began to close and prospectors moved to the new goldfields. Shops, hotels and other buildings were abandoned.

Nearly a hundred years later in 1967, Hill End again came into prominence when it was proclaimed, officially, as a historic site. The old buildings are being maintained and in some cases, as with the Royal Hotel, faithfully restored. The old butcher's shop has been given a new purpose and turned into a restaurant; the old general store is now a trading place for superb country arts and crafts and goodies to eat which include a never-ending supply of local home-made blackberry jam.

Every tourist who ventures out from Sofala along the winding dirt and gravel road (which has changed little since the gold coaches rattled over it a century ago) makes a point of stopping for a drink and a look around the now splendidly restored Hill End pub.

It does brisk business, especially during the weekends and holidays. It is one pub that is perpetually caught by cameras—either early or late in the day when there is no clutter of modern cars and four-wheel drives pulled up out the front and the small herd of cattle that graze on the Hill End Common take a slow toddle through the town's main street.

# The Royal Hotel

## The Broad Arrow Hotel, Broad Arrow, Western Australia

In 1900, the population of the goldmining town of Broad Arrow was 2400. The town had eight hotels, two breweries, a stock exchange and large hospital. These days the population has dwindled to around twenty and there is one hotel. The hotel is one of the original eight and has remained much the same as it was when it was built in 1896.

As with many other pubs, the Broad Arrow can lay claim to having been associated with the making of a film. In 1970 the hotel was featured in *The Nickel Queen*, the first full-length feature film to be made in Western Australia.

The area around Broad Arrow was a burrower's paradise in the 1890s when everyone had a touch of goldfever. The town sprang up in 1893 and was named after a prospector who wanted to make sure his mates would follow him— so he marked his tracks with arrows one metre long scratched into the dirt ...

Rex Newell was in the bar of the Broad Arrow being told the story of how the town came by its name when bar service was required next to him by a couple of old-timers who wandered in. As is the nature of pubs, conversations are easily overheard, and this one, unforgettably so.

'Poor old Bert's dead,' said one fellow.

'Yeah,' said the second. 'In Leonora yesterday ...'

'Bloody shame. Poor old Bert ...'

'Yeah ...'

'What'd he die of?'

'Dunno. But it wasn't very serious ...'

Newell managed *not* to bite a chunk out of the glass from which he was drinking *and* to keep a straight face.

# The Broad Arrow Hotel

# The Railway Hotel, Koorawatha, New South Wales

In the early days, appropriately perhaps, Koorawatha was called Bang Bang. It was the place where bushranger Ben Hall made good his escape after an attempt to steal horses from a local inn in 1864.

They still like to recount the yarn at the Railway Hotel, which stands impressively on a corner site on Olympic Way, twenty-seven kilometres from Cowra and forty kilometres from Young. A two-storeyed brick and iron-roofed building, little of its history seems to be known, but locals insist that Ben called in for a fortifying pint at the Railway before embarking on his horse-thieving attempt which involved a fair amount of gunplay.

The hotel has had many alterations. As Bang Bang grew, so did the public bar. In 1959 fire gutted one part of the large L-shaped pub. The burnt area was not replaced but razed and converted into a beer garden. A new iron roof was necessary after the fire and the building of this did not effect business. It carried on as usual but in a novel way—from the hotel's stables which are still standing and in good repair.

The hotel's various licensees have been mystified by the two unusual windows at the cockies' (cow cockies or graziers) end of the bar. Encompassing the hotel's doors they are shaped like enormous railway tunnels and this is construed as a deliberate architectural touch to give a meaningful and unique effect to yet another Railway Hotel.

# The Railway Hotel

# The Willawarrin Hotel, Willawarrin, New South Wales

Nineteen miles out of Kempsey in the mountains on the road to Bellbrook stands the Willawarrin Hotel, known affectionately by the locals as the 'Warrin'. Around the turn of the century, Willawarrin was an important staging place for travellers to Armidale and in 1905 the first Willawarrin Hotel was built by John Carey to accommodate them. A large welcoming lantern was a main feature of the entrance to the pub above the spacious verandah.

As a young fellow, Rex Newell spent many a night at the Willawarrin. It was a popular haunt on a Friday night. Newell recalls many local bushmen and property owners arriving there for a session ... hats, dogs and all. Another reason why the Warrin was popular was 'Peter Kerr's pies'.

Newell spent a lot of time yarning at the pub with a friend, Reg Hudson, the one and only local mechanic at Willawarrin who owned the one and only garage. Newell said, 'He told me, and plenty of others, a story about the local Aborigines who live in nearby Bellbrook and how on their way through town they'd stop at Reg's garage and ask "Hey mate, you got any second-hand oil?"

'Reg used to save the old oil from cars before refilling with new oil and he'd always give it to the Aborigines upon request. One day after giving a tin full of "second-hand oil" to an Aboriginal man, the fellow turned to Reg and asked, "You got any second-hand petrol?"

'The story got around fairly quickly and after that it became a ritual as soon as Reg walked into the Warrin for someone to ask him if he had any "second-hand petrol" to give us.'

WILLAWARRIN HOTEL 1905

# The Willawarrin Hotel

## The Moonan Flat Hotel, Moonan Flat, New South Wales

When Rex Newell was in the bar of the Moonan Flat Hotel, the talk was of the art of horsemanship and of rough riding, steer wrestling and calf roping. The Australian Rough Riders' Association was putting on its annual rodeo at nearby Scone in a few days' time.

Newell, with a minimal knowledge of horsemanship, did a lot of listening as the names and accomplishments of some of the great riders unfolded until the question was put to him by one of the locals, 'How do you stop a horse pigrooting?'

'Wouldn't have a clue, mate,' Newell said, shaking his head.

'Shoot the pig!' was the reply.

The entire bar roared with laughter.

On his travels around Australia to paint pubs, Rex Newell became accustomed to the wit and humour that surfaced in bars. He is sorry he didn't have a tape recorder handy to get every good joke that emerged but confesses to being like most other people ... hearing and appreciating good jokes that go in one ear and out the other.

'THE OLD COCKEY AT THE BACK OF THE PUB'

# The Moonan Flat Hotel

## The Surveyor-General Inn, Berrima, New South Wales

In 1820 Surveyor James Harper was sent south of Sydney to measure early land grants but due to illness, retired and settled in Berrima where he built his brick home in 1834 and the Surveyor-General Inn which he named after Surveyor-General, Sir Thomas Mitchell.

The hotel claims to be Australia's oldest continually licensed inn but many authorities disagree with this, stating that it is even inaccurate to refer to it as the oldest continually licensed inn in New South Wales. It is known that the George IV or Royal George Hotel, Picton, was established in 1819 and the Macquarie Arms, Windsor, in 1814; and soon after the Macquarie Arms, the Bush Inn and the New Norfolk, near Hobart, Tasmania, were opened. Others claim that our oldest inn is the Mason's Arms, set up in Parramatta in 1796. It later moved across the road and ultimately changed its name to the Wool Pack Inn and the change of address rules it out as being the nation's oldest continually licensed hotel on the one spot.

In the minds of many though, it is the Surveyor-General that holds the title. Constructed in sandstone, the two-storeyed inn was built by Harper in the same year that he built his home. He was the first licensee and the business remained in the Harper family for three generations. The family finally parted with the pub in 1924.

There have been some alterations to the hotel, certainly to the exterior walls with the removal of the lime plaster that once covered irregularities. The verandah has been much altered and although the building has an impressively early historical date, many consider it has lost forever the patina of age.

Located on the Hume Highway nine kilometres south of Mittagong and nine kilometres west of Moss Vale and Bowral, it draws not only tourists and travellers but a stack of noted media personalities, sportsmen and skiers (in the winter months).

## The Victoria Hotel, Hinton, New South Wales

Hinton had its beginnings with a sale of a hundred allotments of land in 1840. A wharf was built in 1844 and over the next thirty years the town went ahead and many substantial buildings appeared. But competition with other river trade on the Hunter combined with the 1890s Depression halted further growth almost completely.

The town has lapsed into obscurity to the extent that it does not appear on many maps. The nearby town of Morpeth and the city of Maitland are far better known.

'THE CARD PLAYERS'

# The Victoria Hotel

# The Commercial Hotel, Braidwood, New South Wales

If there is one Commercial Hotel in Australia, there are hundreds. At Braidwood, New South Wales, locals have dubbed their Commercial Hotel, the 'Comical' because of its happy atmosphere. One barmaid has sworn she will never leave the 'Comical' because she'd miss the laughs. She wants to stay there—and die laughing!

Happy atmospheres don't just happen—they are created. Frank and Winifred Raynolds had run the pub for almost fifteen years when Rex Newell decided to paint it and include it in his pub portfolio. They were held to be largely responsible for the warm, happy atmosphere at the Commercial. Landholders in the area for some time, they patronised and loved the pub so much that they finally bought it. When not serving behind the bar, Frank happily dons his barbecue apron and cooks steaks and bakes fish for patrons.

The pub's best-loved feature is the big, open fireplace in the bar which certainly promotes cosiness on raw winter's nights in southern New South Wales. The pub is a double-storeyed brick building (plastered and painted on the outside) which smacks of old age. No alterations have ever been made to it—only plumbing improvements inside.

Shearers, graziers and truckies are pub regulars. Trading is always brisker on cattle sale days and rodeos and polocrosse tournaments mean extra visitors.

Various buildings in the area were used as settings for the filming of *Ned Kelly* and regulars at the 'Comical' became quite used to Mick Jagger (who played Ned) calling in for a daily pint of ale. Happily Jagger left his guns and armour behind and his visits, unlike those of the dinky-di Ned, were not prone to cause chaos.

BRAIDWOOD 1977

# The Commercial Hotel

# The Hero of Waterloo Hotel, Sydney, New South Wales

The historic Rocks area occupies a small slice of land on the western side of Sydney Cove and was the scene of the colourful beginnings of this nation. Named after the jagged rocks early sailors had to scramble across to reach land, the area is now a busy, vital centre of commerce and tourism. Art galleries, craft centres, specialty shops, showrooms, restaurants and hotels are included.

Owners of businesses and their staffs are aware of how unique the location is and have covered the face of their businesses with a veneer of nostalgia. One of the main focal points of the Rocks is the Hero of Waterloo Hotel. It is thought to be Sydney's oldest operating hotel and was built by George Paton in 1833-34 and licensed in 1845.

The hotel is never short of clever buskers or musical entertainers who hope for generous donations from the many passing tourists.

The large sign out the front of the hotel states the name, 'The Hero of Waterloo', and includes a large painted portrait of the hero. It hangs from a big iron frame over the front door which also formerly held oil lamps which were required by law in earlier days to guide travellers.

Small wonder that when Margaret and John McKinlay bought a derelict pre-Federation house across the road from the pub some years back and decided to restore it and turn a portion of it into an art gallery, they named the gallery after the hero of Waterloo and called the place the Duke of Wellington.

# The Hero of Waterloo Hotel

## The Harbord Beach Hotel, Harbord, New South Wales

Built in 1928 by Hope Katen, the Harbord Beach Hotel was based on the design of a guest house that Katen once stayed in on the island of Samoa. The public bar held about twenty people and the saloon bar about twelve people.

Opposite the hotel were tennis courts for the guests. Weekends were the busiest times for the hotel: people often arrived by tram from Manly.

One of the famous people who frequented the hotel was Peter Dawson, the tenor. Fred Lussick was publican from 1944 to 1954.

MANLY HARBORD TRAM 1930

# The Harbord Beach Hotel

# The Pub With No Beer, Taylors Arm, New South Wales

Christened the unlikely name of the Cosmopolitan Hotel, the Pub With No Beer on the North Coast of New South Wales has had a colourful history. Riding with the good and bad times of the district, the hotel has served locals, and later tourists, since the turn of the century. Built by a German immigrant, J. H. Huttman, the Cosmopolitan started life in 1896 as a boarding house (now the hotel's old living quarters) and began trading as a hotel after additional building work in 1903. The building has changed little in its eighty-five years.

The hotel has been the centre of some controversy in recent years concerning its new title 'the Pub With No Beer'. Apparently a pub in Queensland laid claim to the title, but the dispute was resolved and the residents of Taylors Arm can rest assured that theirs is the genuine article.

Incidentally, the name hails from a song written by Gordon Parsons and recorded by Slim Dusty in the sixties. The resulting tourist trade has been phenomenal and at Easter each year thousands flock to this tiny community of one hundred for the annual music festival held in the grounds of the hotel.

While imbibing a drink or two at the Pub With No Beer customers can also learn a lot about the history of the region. Largely the work of John and Ella White, who ran the pub from 1973–87, the pub now holds a mini-museum within its walls with photographs and relics from the days of old.

# The Pub With No Beer

## The Warialda Rail, Warialda, New South Wales

The town of Warialda lies in the centre of a rich pastoral region in northern New South Wales. Warialda Rail is a railway siding 7 kilometres from Warialda.

Today there are only three buildings standing at Warialda Rail— the old railway siding, the general store and the hotel. Called the Warialda Rail, the hotel is affectionately known as the Gully Pub by the locals who insist that the pub is doing brisk business.

'SATURDAY AT THE GULLY PUB'

# The Warialda Rail

## The Gurley Hotel, Gurley, New South Wales

It is most appropriate that there should be a hotel at Gurley, which is situated twenty kilometres south of Moree on the Narrabri road—the name Moree comes from an Aboriginal word meaning 'a waterhole'. The Gurley Hotel is a very welcome waterhole in this district, which has frequent heatwaves in summer and long dry spells. The annual rainfall is only 578 millimetres per year.

` THE DROVERS

# The Gurley Hotel

# The Ironbark Inn, Stuart Town, New South Wales

Stuart Town is located in the Western Plains region of New South Wales, on the railway line between Orange and Dubbo.

## The Ironbark Inn

For years now, I've been visiting a  place called Stuart Town
And stopping for a cold beer, at the pub;
The Ironbark Inn they call it, with concrete wall to wall,
A kind of rough, good-humoured country club.
The Hannelleys and the Stanfords, the Frappells and the Langs,
The Dickersons, the Edwards, and the Hursts;
I've had a beer with all of them, and I'll have some more,
Even though our wives have often cursed.

This funny little country pub, this hub of social life,
Where all the locals gather for a beer,
So worshipped by the menfolk, so hated by their wives,
It has an almost magic atmosphere.
I've had a beer with Priests and Popes, with Policemen, Politicians,
With businessmen who've come up for the ride;
And none of us has felt ashamed, for we can always say,
That when we drank, we always drank with Pryde.

I wasn't born in Stuart Town, but how I love that place,
And I accept, I'll never be a local,
But I like to sing the praises and tell a yarn or two,
And in my cups, become a poet vocal.
The trouble is, I lose all track of time, and get home late,
To a wife who's understandably annoyed;
So should I be in Stuart Town with limits on my time,
The Ironbark Inn's the one place I avoid.

There's not too many people left in Stuart Town today,
It's mostly quiet— some tourists call it 'cute',
It's known for sheep and cattle, for the Mookerawa State Park,
For turning out the country's finest fruit.
It used to be a mining town, when Gold was God, they say,
Now it's quite a goldmine for the purists
Seeking local history— the locals don't mine gold—
they're much too busy mining all the tourists.

Once they called it Ironbarks, you all recall the rhyme,
When Banjo Paterson immortalised
That fellow with the whiskers, who took the barber on?
And thumped those city youths he so despised.
Having known the people, living there today,
I'm pretty certain some must be descended
From Banjo's doughty hero of many years ago,
When he wrote about that barber's battle splendid.

They're mostly all clean-shaven now, there are some beards about,
But the spirit of the town remains the same:
They're a tough and 'doing' people, able to survive,
Worthy of that famous Ironbarks name.
No matter what they call it, Ironbarks or Stuart Town,
No matter what the future may arrange,
When I come out to Stuart Town, to have a beer or two,
I pray the Ironbark Inn will never change.

From *The First Clip* by Blue the Shearer, printed by Masterprint Pty Ltd, Dubbo, New South Wales, 1979.

# The Ironbark Inn

## The Bellbird Hotel, Bellbird, New South Wales

Located about thirty kilometres west of Newcastle, the charming little town of Bellbird developed around the colliery that was built there in 1908. The two-storeyed Bellbird Hotel was once alive with miners relaxing over a few beers after a hard day's work.

# The Bellbird Hotel

## The Club Hotel, Emmaville, New South Wales

At the time Rex Newell painted the Club, Alex Johnson, a seventy-four-year-old grave-digger and experienced tin-fossicker, was the pub's leading personality.

Alex constantly livened up the bar with his yarns and one that never failed to delight concerned his coming in to Emmaville from a tin-fossicking stint on a Friday night which was traditionally a 'spruce up' occasion for men. The town barber was so drunk that Alex took over the operation— drinking solidly as he shaved beards and cut hair. Clients drank likewise. Alex did such a hatchet job that the next morning nobody recognised each other. Everyone presumed everyone else to be a stranger and the Club bar was wall-to-wall with fights!

The town loves the story of Alex going to Glen Innes, accompanied by his granddaughter Wendy to buy a new car. Asked by the car salesman as to his next-of-kin or closest relative, Alex thought for a bit and replied: 'It must be Wendy. She's standing right next to me!'

Publicans like the Club. It has been operating now for just on 110 years and in that time has had only four owners. It is a single-storeyed colonial timber building on to which an additional section was added in 1910 from bricks kilned locally at Emmaville. The present owners won't admit to sitting on a 'gold mine' but they are hoping an earth-tremor never strikes Emmaville. The whole of the pub's backyard has been mined in the past and there is a honeycomb of disused tunnels running under the hotel.

MINERS GRAVES' EMMAVILLE

# The Club Hotel

# The Stop Over Pub, somewhere in the Outback

Rex Newell has painted this pub as one representing those in the bush that accommodated the horse-drawn coaches.

Our earliest bush pubs were little more than rough grog shops set up in bark huts where a teamster driving bullocks could rest after perhaps a day's journey of around twelve kilometres.

When the horse-drawn era took over in the 1850s, more substantial buildings went up to cater for passengers staying overnight. To spell the horses, a fresh team would be put in between the traces for the next leg of the journey.

The early inland road routes tended to follow rivers and creeks because both horses and working bullocks needed water. (Later, cars continued to follow in the tracks of the coaches on the same road services which were gradually improved. This is why so many highways are subject to flooding.)

Although there were other outfits operating coach lines, the one name that stands out is that of Cobb & Co. For seventy years, its 'wobblies' clattered across the outback. It seems hardly believable that these coaches were still servicing areas of central and northern Queensland as late as 1924 when the last Cobb & Co. coach was taken out of service. Motor cars were, by then, travelling the outback (although not in any great numbers) and Qantas had started its airline operations in 1921. The rail lines had snaked out of many outback areas, and had gradually led to the decline of the coaching business.

There are still old-timers around who have seen transport change from horse-drawn coach to space flight. It may be assumed that just as an astronaut is happy to get back to base, the passengers on coaches were always glad when the driver quitted the box seat, downed the ribbons and pulled up at a stop over.

# The Stop Over Pub

# Index